Little Boy

Matthew Chanan-Khan

BRIDGE LOGOS
Newberry, FL 32669

Bridge-Logos, Inc.
Newberry, FL 32669

Little Boy: A Poetic Voyage Through Teenage Mental Health
by Matthew Chanan-Khan

Copyright© 2025 by Matthew Chanan-Khan

All rights reserved. Under International Copyright Law, no part of this publication may be reproduced, stored, or transmitted by any means—electronic, mechanical, photographic (photocopy), recording, or otherwise—without written permission from the publisher and copyright holder.

Library of Congress Catalog Card Number: 2025949174

International Standard Book Number: 978-1-61036-925-1

International Standard Book Number: 979-8815-0968-2

Interior Layout and Cover Design:
Ashley Morgan | GraphicGardenLLC@gmail.com

*This book is dedicated
to my father on earth,
Asher Chanan-Khan, and
my Father in Heaven.
Thank you for guiding
me through the long dark
nights of my soul.*

Contents

Preface v

Apathetic Heart 1
The Prodigal Inside of Us 3
What Does It Mean? 5
Recovery, I Need. 6
What Does It Mean to Be Yours? 8
Dopamine 10
Unbelief 12
Relationships 14
Stranded 16
How Do You Trust Your Mind? 18
See You in Heaven 20
Titanic 21
Away. 22
Chemicals Don't Work for Me. 23
Myth. 25
The Exchange (Shalom). 26
Apologies (Family) 27

Somebody Else 28
Not Worth Looking For 29
Need You to Care 30
Trust Issues........................... 31
Hiding in Your Blues 33
Enough?................................ 34
Conversation with The Past............ 35
Time to Find Yourself 37
Suicide................................ 38
Pain of the Dark 39
Little Boy............................. 40
Where I'm Cared About................. 41
Protected?............................. 43
Hypocrite.............................. 45
I'm Sorry for Who I Am................ 46
Man of Sorrows......................... 47
Where Do I Go? 48
Hard Drive............................. 49
Vulnerable............................. 50
Closed Door............................ 51
In Truth............................... 52
A Restoration Ballad 53

Preface

THERE I WAS. Trembling in the emergency room of Wolfson Children's Hospital. A purgatory of what was to come. The nurse approached my room and uttered the dreaded phrase, "Come with me." Snatching my belongings, including my phone, the sole means of contact to the outside world, she seated me in a wheelchair. Tears trickling down my cheeks, legs anxiously shaking, I couldn't help but ask why and to where I was being taken. I wasn't disabled or impaired. Or was I? The doctors, psychiatrists, and my own dear parents would determine that on my behalf.

I soon arrived at my destination within the Wolfson Psychiatry Department. Still frightened and fearful, the nurse wheeled me through a door with a sign that read, *Wolfson Psychiatric Ward*. I lost sight of my parents' worried faces as I entered through the God-forsaken door that might potentially determine my fate for the next few months. As I entered this hallway, eyes of different kids judgmentally stared me down as if I was an unknown outsider that did not belong. What they didn't know is that I too felt like an outsider. The nurse led me to a room with bed and a desk where I lay down heart-shattered, terrified, and alone.

I abide in this psychologic jail cell, and I feel like I'm going insane. I try to think of peaceful thoughts, but my tranquil imagination dissipates, and it seems then as if my mind is endlessly spiraling out of control. It may appear as if this solitary confinement will, to some degree, assuage the psychological duress I endure but it instead trapped me inside my mind. Every ounce of depression in my body painted the barren walls of this room and now I was confined and reminded of the living hell of my mental health.

After a few hours of immersion in the depressive distress that encapsulated my room, I was approached by a familiar figure. The psychiatrist entered my room and began by asking the cliché questions designated for a mentally ill patient. "How are you feeling? Are there any problems at home that have caused these emotions? Do you know why you're here?" I pleaded with the psychiatrist to not imprison me in this ward for months. He simply replied, "I'll see what I can do." Hopelessly, I fell onto the rock-hard bed in despair awaiting my dreaded fate.

I arose from my bed of false comfort when the nurse entered my room. She said, "Come with me." I followed her anxiously, perturbed by what will happen to me. My mind continued to spiral out of control as I approached the room with the doctor and my parents. As I entered, they stood up and I saw an indescribable expression on their faces as I stared at them ashamed of myself. The psychiatrist spoke, "Matthew, you are free to go." The words hit me, and suddenly a weight left my chest. It was as if I

PREFACE

was to some degree temporarily freed from this pain. I proceeded to gather my belongings and exit the hospital to which my gratitude for the world and life itself exponentiated because of this close experience with true solitary confinement.

This book is a collection of poems and ballads I had written throughout the early teenage years of my life. I wrote these days, months, and years following this event in my life. While still enjoyable, these years had overwhelmed me with trials and tribulations. Heartbreak, fear, pain, depression, and grief are some of the themes in this poetic journey through my struggle with mental health as a teenager. My hope and prayer for this book is that those facing mental hardships and torment will feel heard, empathized, and hopeful that they will conquer this mental mountain and enjoy life unbounded from this pain and suffering.

Apathetic Heart

Are you scarred,
My apathetic heart?
You've got a thousand bullets blow
surrounding you are endless shards
causing hurt wherever you go

But do you care,
My apathetic heart?
so much pain that you are not even scared
in fact, you wake yourself up to be prepared
you have an army to embrace all the hurt and despair

My apathetic heart
you're so numb inside, and dark
you apathetic soul
don't you care if you're made whole?
You, apathetic mess
so indifferent to your brokenness

Why so numb,
My apathetic heart?
broken down and you feel like you have none
does your life seem like it has been hung?
before a fighting chance, it surrendered and took a plunge

Do you want hope,
My apathetic heart?
or would you rather just live in misery?
do you not want to be emotionally free?
leave your past and find your liberty

LITTLE BOY

I know it's hard,
My apathetic heart
the ties of the past are quite dark
left my wounded heart with eternal scars
but I know a surgeon whose touch heals this apathetic heart

The Prodigal Inside of Us

I know I am a sinful man
I know my life is in the sinking sand
I know I am a prodigal
But I am making my way back home

This is a long and dusty road
No sign from the Holy Ghost
I am covered in this filthiness
Quite the opposite of righteousness

I ran away from my Holy God
Straight to the devil is how I flawed
Committed my life to wickedness
How could I escape from all this sickness?

I return to the ornate and divine palace
The last place where I should ever be
Ought to be chained for blasphemy
Or killed for my unrighteousness

Yet, I am embraced with a hug
And a kiss on the forehead for this messed-up thug
Wrapped around in His holy gown
My sin does no longer abound

There's a prodigal inside, at our core
But God only looks down with love for sure
Even when I screw up a million times more
His love won't change my entire life assured

LITTLE BOY

I am sorry for my wicked ways
I am sorry for all those shameful days
Please turn this stone into a beating heart
God, please keep me close and do not depart

What Does It Mean?

I have been trying for so long
To find a place where I belong
I have been searching all my life
To find somewhere I can abide

I have been looking out my window
Trying to change that I am solo
I am trying to keep my distance
But I no longer can bear this loneliness

What does it mean to be alone?
What does it mean to have a home?
What does it mean to find peace in your circumstances?
What does it mean to have a friend?
What does it mean for God to mend?
All the fractures that are found in my heart

I have been trying for some time
To check out of this life
I have been trying to numb all this pain
But all I did is exacerbate

What does it mean to find the one?
What does it mean for that to be God?
What does it mean to hold His hand, along the way?
What does it mean to trust His Word?
When you're drowning in your hurt
What does it mean to know that God is still your friend?

Can I trust that He will be my friend?

Recovery, I Need

I don't think I am doing it your way
I keep running thousand miles astray
I can't let my life decay
Cause I am done running miles away

So, help me recover
Then help me discover
The one true God
Help me recover
Help me discover
What it means to be your son

I don't think we are on the same path
I don't think that it is my God that I have
My life doesn't reflect the Christian man
Probably don't know, is it with the devil I stand

Help me recover help me discover
What it means to be your child
Help me recover help me discover
What it means to regain my fire

I know that I want to be on God's path
The only problem is my heart's split in half
I say I'm all in with this whole religious God thing
But the key to unlock it, is the faith I don't have

RECOVERY, I NEED

Help me encounter
Don't let me be devoured
Keep me safe in your righteous hand
I know I don't believe
But help me to see
That God it was you who was my first love

What Does It Mean to Be Yours?

Faith is too hard
Too many conflictions
Faith is what I have lost
No godly decisions

God is off my charts
He's missing in action
I am falling apart
But then, was he ever present?

What does it mean to be loved?
What does it mean to know God?
What does it mean to trust in his Word?
What does it mean to give Him your all?
Cede your heart at the cross
I'd kill myself, just to know that you are there?

And kill myself to just know you care

I am so far
From that holy destination
I am so lost
From that moral position

I am a rogue
That's on a mission
To regain my faith
In need of a holy visitation

WHAT DOES IT MEAN TO BE YOURS?

I need my God
But I don't know if he exists
I look at the cross
But still, I am but a skeptic

What's wrong with my heart
Why can't I accept it?
My mind doesn't know the truth
Still God, please let it be You

Dopamine

Birds singing as they fly
The peace and quiet of the night
Singing songs by the fire
The peacefulness has arrived

Kids swimming in the ocean
Innocence in every motion
Loving every moment that passes by
Oh, how it feels to be swinging high

I am hoping
To regain that child's dopamine
I am hoping
To enjoy all these pleasant things
I am hoping
To find peace in life's simplicity
I am hoping
That what I'll find is tranquility

Casting lines by the dock
Watching the flight of some hawks
Admiring God's creation
This is my go-to ideation

Reading Scripture at sunrise
Then sleeping under night sky
Watching this beautiful life
Am I content in the high life?

DOPAMINE

Am I content in all of this?
Is this the peak of my satisfaction?
Is the simple life that I am looking for
Or is there more, behind the spiritual door?

Unbelief

Why don't you speak when I yell for you,
Why are you silent when I vent my blues
I'm here! trying to serve you God!
Yet you'll answer to the ones that aren't

Can't you take this away from me
The doubt, that questions who you are?
And if you can why do you not God?
And show me your heart that you are not far

You say you'll never leave,
But your presence is the void I see
All I seek is some reprieve,
But it's you God that's missing from me

So, what can I do to believe
In you, the way you believe in me?
God I'm yours and I will surrender now
All glory is yours, teach me that somehow

Are you real?
Are you there?
God, will you show me that you care?

I'm on my knees, I'm crying loud,
Lord, so much I need you now,

Lord, take this cup from me
Because, Jesus, you are all I seek,
All I need is your relief,
Lord, come now and help my unbelief

UNBELIEF

My head aches, my heart breaks,
My soul yearns for you, oh my Lord
You say that you will heal my every scar
And give me the faith to trust who you are

So grant me the faith in who you are,
Take all my scars and give me a whole heart

Relationships

I've got a strained relationship with God
a healthy love, that's not what I got
A mental state that does not determine my fate
I am at a loss because of all my pain

I cannot stop my overthinking now
Because I don't trust what comes out of their mouths
I can't even trust what God has ever said
Because all I hear are lies in the Book I read

I have a hard time keeping you close
I have a hard time with the l-o-v-e I know
I wish those four letters meant a bit more,
What is love? I think I will never know

They tell me that God is truly love
That all the good things, they come from above
But when I look at my situation
All I feel is God's deviation

My friends say I overthink way too much
They ask to slow down, just trying to keep up
I am sorry my mind races like a car
I don't mean to, but I can't help going too far

I struggle with my faith every single day
Caught in doubts I can't allay
I want to keep you all close and near
But honestly, my heart and mind are unclear

RELATIONSHIPS

I don't want to overthink or doubt
But that's the way my living's all about
Truth is, I'm scared to be betrayed
And lose the friends I have made

I'm scared that everyone will go
I'm scared that my loneliness will only grow
Like God, my friends too may fade away
And I'll be left to endure my mind's decay

Stranded

I can't bear it anymore
As I weep on the shores
Of mercy through the night of strife
I can't see me anymore
I am covered with mental sores
Incurable and stranded on the land

Of no more

Help me with my unbelief
It's a sinking ship at the sea
I lost my anchor now

I am stuck fighting an endless strife
Of (my) mental spirituality fights
I need you by my side

I am stressing, I need you with me here
I need you to draw near
But you are off my radar now

My compass won't even work
I am drowning in this island's dirt
I can't see a way out of this

And I'm conflicted all the time
Through every journey in my life
I can't seem to understand the truth
I think it's walked away from me
Because now I'm lost at sea
If I find truth, I surely will be free

STRANDED

I am still here calling in my own mayday
I know I'm not okay
I just need to be saved

So, come here and bring me peace of mind
Be the friend oh God most high
We'll sail through the seas

I am not stuck in the waves
In emotional spiritual pain
I know that he will come and save
It's still hard to go and trust
But that is faith so I must
I can trust he'll hear my S.O.S.

How Do You Trust Your Mind?

How do you trust your mind,
When it is in constant fright?
How do you trust your own mind
When it doesn't know the dark from the light.

Why can't I sleep at night?
All I seem to do is continue to cry,
Why can't I be alright,
I don't know, but I must try,

It is unfortunate
I have got depression
Life gave me lots of hits
Makes me want to quit
I am suicidal
That's my idol
I fantasize
About my demise

I want to give away my life
Due to the stress of my mind
I want to give away my life
I don't care I run out of time

My friends say to keep my life
If I do, I'll run away and hide
Run to the outskirts, run outside
But then I stay cooped up
And all I do is cry

HOW DO YOU TRUST YOUR MIND?

I guess I will stay alive
Even though my mind will die
I guess I will stay alive
But for what purpose I will never know why

See You in Heaven

I am trapped in a cave
I'm fighting with my shame
I am thinking of the life I chose to live

I am thinking of my loved ones
But would they care at all
I can't pursue my mental brawl
No more burdens I wish to haul

No more oxygen do I want
I am done with it all
Or the people, I can call

See you in heaven my friend
Not on earth, that's come to an end
See you in heaven my friend
It's time to give up on trying to mend

I was asking for help
For my mental health
Sorry I shut you out
But who do you care about

All the stuff I went through
Just to find my own blues
Melancholia's a disease of the heart that ache
Makes me stop my breath, with my life at stake

Titanic

It's time to let the ship sail
Time to embrace my life's ending trail
Time to see the ship go down
It's time for me sink and drown

An iceberg is seen up ahead
Those are the traumas of my mental health
Thought I could avoid the hurting past
But the peace in my heart could never last

The water filled all these souls
The time to live has got to go
I want to try and save myself
That's the lost cause of my mental health

So, you can try to give me a helping hand
But truly I am too far out from the land
Don't know how to survive or to keep my life
From the thoughts of me wanting to die

Away

I'm going to run, runaway
Going to fly, flyaway
From the man I became
Take a break from all the pain

I need to clean my spiritual mess
Or evade more and more stress
Could I take that horrid pill?
To gain the eternal tranquil

Would this lead to my demise?
But does it get worse than my current state of life
I need to stop all my lying
My feelings are all that I am hiding

I'll hide and find a cave
Away from my shame
I'll rest and be alone
Where myself I'll never have to show

Chemicals Don't Work for Me

Chemicals don't work for me
They can't even set me free
They're here then they're gone
I feel I don't belong
I am left with my drug

Chemicals don't set me free
I am chained, and I'm on my knees
A slave, I am an addict
Here I am trapped in
My self-pity

Because I am looking for love
Looking for hope
Looking for a home to not be alone
Looking for peace
Looking to keep
A relationship with God

I am in an addict's house
Lost with no God around
Lonely and in hell
Under a spell
Of my mental health

Bound by invisible chains
Chemicals just work that way
Walking and maundering
Depressed and I'm pondering
Who I really am

But I am beating me down

LITTLE BOY

No one to surround
As I tarnish my mental house
So, help me God
So, I do not
Ruin You and me for the rest of my life

Chemicals don't set me free
But I'm hoping God will help me see
I am praying, I am crying
Feels like I am dying
But I know He will save.

Myth

No one understands me
Not even myself
They see me as a broken man
Struggling with his mental health

"You are fine" is what I hear
Hide your stress behind those tears
You're okay, it doesn't exist
Because your depression is but a myth

Happier, you need to be
I don't see your anxiety
"You're okay, it doesn't exist"
Because your depression is but a myth

But I am a broken dark man
No love to be had
Always told to shut up
And stop being sad

It's all in your head
Some piled up with stress
The pain of my mind
In a mental prison cell

"You are fine" is all I hear
I'll hide my stress and my fears
Am I okay? Should I even exist?
Because my depression is but a myth.

The Exchange (Shalom)

Shalom Shalom
The peace of God is with us
Shalom Shalom
His peace becomes our home

Shalom
Shalom

I know it's hard being mentally unwell
I know it hurts being in a mental hell
I know you are tired, you hurt, you weep
Come take this joy and more you'll reap

I know the mind races on several paths
I know your heart's broken, forever sad
I know you feel lost and want to seek
A joy where it is God you keep

Give me your burdens
I'll give you my yoke
Give me your sorrow
I'll give you a home
Give me your trauma
Let it all go
give me your heart
And you'll make a new start

Apologies (Family)

My loving family, I apologize, I ask for your grace
For losing my heart, that now I cannot replace
My mental health turned love into an empty space
And then left me in this broken place

Oh, our lives were filled with laughter
We were all happy
Broken hearts aren't shattered
But filled with tranquility

Then I had the breakdown, the final straw
A tipping point, my mind tormented with flaws
A soul turned inside out, completely torn apart
My unhealthy mind holding a broken heart

Then you all came rushing in
To witness my calamity within
At the expense of my own suffering
I let you all see the punishing sin

I won't be vulnerable
I don't want you to fret
We'll all be happier with my feeling tucked aside
Only if I can face the vicious storms I cannot hide

I know we are now tarnished
We are all destroyed
I showed you my sadness that took away God's joy
I haven't been the best, my soul is in pain
I am sorry, inside my chest only sorrow remains
We are all now ruined, because of my mental health

Somebody Else

I can't look myself in the mirror
I can't wipe these tired sad eyes
I can't get myself to draw nearer
To the lonely boy that cries at night

I want to be new
I want to be changed
I don't ever want to be the same

I want to be somebody else
I want to drown this ugly self
I want to find somewhere to escape
I never want to be the same

I can't look at my inward self
But who am I kidding, no one looks at me
And I know that I am depressed
But I conclude I cannot be free

Is it heaven or earth
The sky or the dirt
Where I really want to be

Is it heaven or earth
Sky or dirt
But will my chains follow me

Not Worth Looking For

I know these are depressing
You want less pessimism
So, I'll give you what you want at my expense

You know joy is still hard to get
It's not a snap of your fingers, there it is
It's like waiting on divine promises

Don't go looking
To be loved
Don't go searching
To be enough
Don't go finding
Approval
No one loves your lonely soul

They say that sadness is a scent
That leaves you friendless at the end
Then I am alone without a forever friend

I don't really understand love
It's not simple, will I ever be enough?

Need You to Care

I've been devoid of friendship
I've been devoid of love
Devoid of holding God's hand
And hearing Him say that "I am enough"

It seems that I am alone
Solitude that's my home
I've been the gruff lone wolf
That in his sadness has lost his soul

I need you in the sunrise
I need you when my mind lies
I need you though I seldom pray
I am awake and
I need you to care

I need you in the dark nights
I need you through my depressing life
I need you when I lost my way
But I don't know if you will care

But God when did you ever show up?
When you saw me lost, sinful and all messed up
I needed your hand holding my face
Instead, I just saw your shadow walk away

Trust Issues

What's going on in my head
It's quite hard to comprehend
I can't even say it aloud

Why would you want to know?
You just leave me here alone
Don't come back yet

To mock me, to maim my heart
Make a show of my mental ill-health
Is that what I am to the world?

And my tears keep falling
My heart keeps wailing
Over the weight inside my chest

I've been alone for most of my life
I've been alone through the hurt and the strife
I don't need you here to wipe away my tears
I'm letting you all go, because you were never here

How do I vocalize
The feeling that I hide
How am I supposed to trust?

Will you be here now in my life?
Through the panic attacks in the night
I doubt you'll ever come

LITTLE BOY

It's not you, you're just fine
But I know that I will lie
If you ask, if I'm okay

I've got these trust issues
That is why I hide my blues
So, you all will leave and go away

Hiding in Your Blues

You don't want to be known
You want to stay alone
Love your life of solitude
You don't need to be shown
A way to smile
So just keep hiding your blues

I live in this cold dark night
My mind in a constant state of fright
I don't know where I have traveled to

But it seems quite comfortable
Hiding all that shame, those stumbles
Could I ever be vulnerable?

This life is quite unhealthy
You've been told by the crowd, by many
I'm telling you it is not - that easy

I'd rather just stay shut up
So, you don't see my tears when I mess up
It's not your fault, it's to your benefit

These ways are not that therapeutic
Not much love, but more condemnation
I just want to go back to a place I've been

Where I'm accepted.

Enough?

I've tried so hard
I've tried to escape the dark
I've tried to be loved
But I know I was never enough

I tried to escape the shame
I tried, but I was always to blame
And I tried with all my might
But it's still hard when you're living in fright

It's been hard
It's been tough
To evade the feeling of not being enough
And I have cried
With my weary brown eyes
Still, I feel the inward heartache and strife

My tears I tried to wipe away
And my heart to disintegrate
Oh, my mind is now - done with it
The question to ask is if I should live?

I have tried to recover
And myself I am yet to discover
This road is long, I don't know where it ends
But it's okay because my heart will mend.

Conversation with the Past

Good times where did you disappear?
Left me longing, trapped in fear
Where did all the joy go?
I'm left here living in woe

My mind captured in this prison cell
a place that feels like hell
God, please don't leave me here
Suffering from my mental fears

But I've been crying for too long
Time to stop, I am done
No more shaking, no more quaking
No more taking, no more breaking
It is time, I am done
I've had enough, no longer can I run

Lonely soul why do you hide?
Where is your truth,
Why are you not by my side?
My tired heart, are you alright?
You see my mental pain through the night

Weary mind is that you?
Can you see past our blues?
Is there something I can do?
Maybe just stay a little longer with you

LITTLE BOY

Thank you for your attempt, I commend
But I think this is permanent, so it must end
We all tried to fix my mental anomalies
But I'm left with yet more fallacies

I guess that's what's wrong with me.

Time to Find Yourself

I've been living in my lies
It's my feelings that I hide
I've been shaking
I've been aching
Trying to find the man taken
and return him to his normal self

It's time to find yourself again
Time to see more than your sin
No looking back at your past
Just keep your eyes up ahead
It's time to find yourself again

I've been locked up in my room
It's a dark, eerie mental tomb
I've been crying
I've been lying
In my head where I've been hiding
To avoid the pain of it all

Now, come out of that tomb
Look in the mirror
It's okay you're safe
Draw nearer
Rest in the arms of love
And know that there's somebody you can trust

It's time to find myself again
Time to see more than just my sin
I won't look back at my past
I'll keep my eyes up ahead
I will find myself again

Suicide

I know you quiver and shake
And I know your heart aches
We are both at breaking points
Let's take it out together

So, what's the point of living
What's the point of being happy
What's the point of life
When you can opt for suicide

I know we all think this
And our boats are sinking
Might as well embrace the change
Of living life in decay

As I write this melody
Body shaking on impending calamity
I can't help but admit
My death's is the world's benefit

Pain of the Dark

I've been traveling alone in deep stress
Struggling through the reigns of my mental illness
It's my self-inflicted wound
A hardship I cannot simply cruise through
How do I ever get out of my blues?

It's a deathly treacherous cold room
A depressing closed capsule, my mental tomb
I wake up in the dark
With a lonely, saddened heart
I'm locked up with my stress from the start

It's time to say goodbye, to my mental tomb
I've had enough of my forever blues
I'll be fine one day in Heaven
Even if it's for a second
Then I will succumb to the pain of my dark

Little Boy

Where did that little boy go?
It's me who I really want to know
Who is this new man I am now?
I want that little boy (back) somehow

Child you were so innocent
Child you were so benevolent
You were the best at being you
But who you are now, I haven't got a clue

Now you are unpredictable
Your emotions, they are so fickle
You are a broken, black-hearted mess
The only definite thing is your stress

I don't know who I am
In this life I don't know where I stand
I want to make a restart
To subtract this darkness in my heart

Where I'm Cared About

I've been neglected
For not opening up
I've been assaulted
By the demons that flood my thoughts

I've been rejected
My health was neglected
So, I made my departure
To a place where they'll accept my heart

So let the fire burn
Let the longing hurt
I will never return to this place, accursed

But the show must go on
When the feelings are numb
Leave my hand in the clouds
I'm flying to a place
Where I'm cared about

Now I am alone here
Filling my cave with tears
Solitude is painful
But I'd rather be here

LITTLE BOY

Let the journey finally cease
So, I can reconcile with peace
Because even when I'm so far out
Let's hope I find a place
Where I'm cared about

Just pray I find a place
where I'm cared about

Protected?

You can see this, yes?
The pain and the weakness
My trials and fears
Will not disappear

My sadness, my shame
Is an ever-growing pain
It wouldn't go away
So, I can't get away

My struggles are right here
They'll bring me to tears
They'll chase me down
like a hound
A vicious predator
Designed for death and murder
Am I protected? Will I be martyred?

My heart is in pieces
The weight of my weakness
I am in its grip
Like a sinking ship

The tide rushes in
It teems up with my sins
I can't get away fast enough
from my past, so tough

LITTLE BOY

Could you hold me tight
Through my treacherous nights
Unblind my eyes
To see the light
So, hold my heart right
Protect it from the dark night
Keep it safe
Away from hate.

Hypocrite

When I talk to you
I feel like a hypocrite
A wretched man
Living a life of sin
A sinking ship
Sailed by a moral hypocrite

I disobeyed every law in the land
How's it possible that here I stand
I disgraced your name
And my tears let go of faith
There's no possibility of my return

I can't get it right I can't see the light
Of the God I pray to with all my might
At church they teach the Heaven you will reach
If you practice what you preach

But I'm a failure
Get it wrong from the start
I'm a failure
Can't change the dark in my heart
I'm a failure
Forever a hypocrite

I'm Sorry for Who I Am

They say the scars don't define
They say if you are in pain, leave it all behind
About your feelings, you don't have to lie
or run away from your problems and hide

God, I'm sorry for who I am
God, I'm sorry for who I am
Come and change me to who I need to be
Come back to me and set this captive free

I feel like an imposter
Where I walk, I trample, I falter
I am different, I'm an outsider
Try to belong, but it really doesn't matter

But in reality, you love all of me
Even my faults and my fallacies
And I'll be fine because you care for me
I'm defined by Your cross and Your reality

Man of Sorrows

I'm alone, I'm a man of sorrows
I'm ashamed of the man I became
I'm alone out here on my own
Where do I go when I maxed out on pain?

So, God renew my soul
Teach this broken heart to be whole
So, God renew my soul
Teach my broken heart to be whole

This life you can't escape it's a strife
It's a war, keep waging your fight
This can pass, even when it seems it never has
But I will trust in the process of God

Help me to love
Help me to trust
Help me to break my cycle of sin, I must
Teach me to heal
Teach me to mend
And surely

Where Do I Go?

Where do I go from here?
Where do I hide carrying all this fear?
Where do I go and cry on my knees?
Where do I seek my lost peace?
Where do I run when I need a home?
Where can I go when I feel alone?
Where am I loved for who I am?
For whom I really am?

My sadness I can't explain
It's an ever-growing pain
It's a war I wage
Every day, but in vain

It's a haunted ghostly spirit
That kills with knives and swords
It's whispers in a ghastly tone
That I'll forever be alone

I'll run right to your arms
In your presence there is no harm
I'll give my cares to you
I know that's true
God, I am safe with you

Hard Drive

I'm telling you that I am alright
Though it may not seem that from the outside
I promise you that I will be fine
I'm just processing my mental hard drive

I know you see me as a quiet man
I'll tell you this isn't who I really am
It's hard to see through my opaque glass
But I am telling you my hurt will pass

I know it may seem that I'm reserved
In truth I'm just healing from the hurt
I know it's confusing to look upon
But I promise these feelings will be gone

Oh, I'm loading my hard drive
Oh, I'm trying to heal from the strife
Oh, I'm changing my state of mind
Might as well fix my entire life

Vulnerable

I've tried to open up
I've tried to give my heart
Tried to let the world see who I really am
But I am scared to be a vulnerable man

My tears in a bottle
Feelings behind the door
They both got a lock but there's no key in store

I don't know what's coming
Or what'll come my way
I need to find a way to preclude pain
I'm done with the heartache
the hurt, the strife, the hate
I need to find a way to keep my heart safe

You try to break the lock
The world's done the same
But when it's opened, all I'll feel is pain

Should I give it a try
Or be reserved all my life
It's not worth the risk of letting anyone come inside

I've tried to open up
I've tried to give my heart
Tried to let the world see who I really am
But I am scared to be a vulnerable man.

Closed Door

Close your mouth
And shut your eyes
And shed your tears into the night
Let the water flow like a river
Pray nobody finds you here
Sitting on the floor in tears
Wishing there was someone that would hold
Because that's why your heart's a closed door

Your heart doesn't like to open up
Your heart will forever remain shut
Your heart can't trust, so nobody comes your way

Because in the past you have been broken, you have been hurt
Like shattered glass
You're left to mend on your own

When they ask
how you're doing?
Why do you always take a pass?
It's like you want to keep on your mask

This masquerade will eventually end
So, God, please welcome me even with my tears
Please teach me how to trust and be near
It's okay to let my guard down when you're near

In Truth

Lately I've been writing a lot of songs
And I am saying, there's got to be something wrong
I don't know what to say, so I will write it all the way
Just please excuse my typical frown

This song is meant to be an explanation
To feed your minds imagination
Of where I devote my time
To what's going on in my mind

So, in truth, in truth
I'm suffering a lot right now
In truth, in truth
My joy has gone down
In truth, in truth
My hearts trapped in a cave
With a lot of lies
And a little faith

I know it's hard to see it
But I want help, I need it
A way to escape from these thoughts
But for a while I probably will not

In truth, in truth
This stage of my life
In truth, in truth
This will all pass by
In truth, in truth
My sadness will have to cease
Time will tell
But I'll be at peace

A Restoration Ballad

I am down on my knees
Crying in agony
I'm down on my knees
Will you help me please?

Because I can't see the sunrise
When my day is in a constant dark
My Joy poses a dim light
And my hope unable to shine

God, I know this may not pass
I'm hoping that Your love will last
I'm counting on your promises
Please don't fail me yet
Because you I need
My need to mend

The light may seem to vanish
But I assure you my faith is never to tarnish
I'll tell you it is temporary
And we'll escape this weary feeling

I know the sun will arise
And my darkness will flee, or it may hide
All my fears and all my tears
Will cease, when He is here

I'll see a new horizon
Across the deep blue glassy sea
Then I know that peace arrived
Come to Him and no longer strive

www.ingramcontent.com/pod-product-compliance
Lightning Source LLC
Chambersburg PA
CBHW061249040426
42444CB00010B/2309